Douglas Florian

An Auto Mechanic

Greenwillow Books, New York

For Haim Lallouz,
master mechanic

Watercolor paints and
pen and ink were used
for the full-color art.
The text type is
Bryn Mawr Book.

Greenwillow Books, a
division of William Morrow
& Company, Inc.,
1350 Avenue of the Americas,
New York, NY 10019.
Printed in Hong Kong
by South China Printing
Company (1988) Ltd.

First Edition
10 9 8 7 6 5 4 3 2 1

Library of Congress
Cataloging-in-Publication Data
Florian, Douglas.
An auto mechanic/by Douglas Florian.
    p.   cm.
Summary: Simple text and
illustrations introduce
the daily work of
an auto mechanic.
ISBN 0-688-10635-8 (tr.)
ISBN 0-688-10636-6 (lib.)
1. Automobile mechanics—
Juvenile literature.
[1. Automobile mechanics.
2. Occupations.]   I. Title.
TL152.F56   1991
629.28′722′023—dc20
90-48809   CIP   AC

An auto mechanic works with cars.

He opens the hood and checks the engine.

He takes off the wheels and checks the brakes.

He changes the oil.

He changes the filters.

air
filter

He fills the radiator with antifreeze.

He fills the tires with air.

He fixes cars with his tools:

wrenches and ratchets,

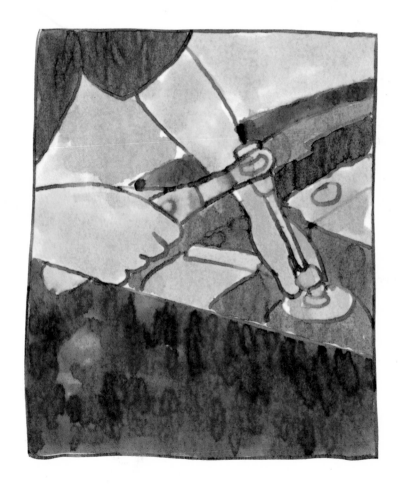

files and funnels,

pullers and pliers,

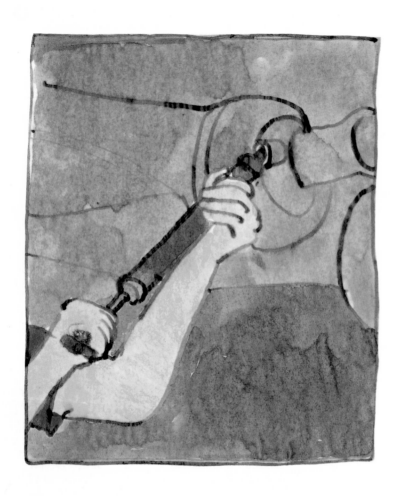 

grease guns and gauges.

Then he tests the engine with a computer.

In his storeroom he keeps spare parts.

In his office he writes bills and orders parts.

All year long,

in his shop or on the road,

an auto mechanic works with cars.